54321 QUIZZES

First published in 2003 by Miles Kelly Publishing Ltd,
Bardfield Centre, Great Bardfield, Essex, CM7 4SL

Copyright © Miles Kelly Publishing Ltd 2003

ISBN 1-84236-278-X

2 4 6 8 10 9 7 5 3 1

Project Manager: Ruthie Boardman
Cover Design: Guy Rodgers

Contact us by email: info@mileskelly.net
Check our website and purchase other Miles Kelly products:
www.mileskelly.net

Printed in Italy

54321
QUIZZES

by
Christopher Rigby

Miles Kelly
PUBLISHING

About the Author

Born in Blackburn, Lancashire in 1960, Christopher Rigby has been compiling and presenting pub quizzes for the past 15 years. When he is not adding to his material for quizzes, Christopher works in the car industry. He is married to Clare – they have two teenage daughters, Hollie and Ashley and share their home with two demented dogs called Vespa and Bailey. A keen Manchester United fan Christopher lists his heroes as George Best and Homer Simpson.

54321 QUIZZES EXPLAINED

The following quiz book comprises of 90 quizzes on a variety of themes. The object of each quiz is to attempt to identify the answer with the help of five clues, which get gradually easier as the points value is reduced. Below is an example.

NAME THE YEAR

5 POINT CLUE In the Democratic Republic of Congo, the town of Goma was engulfed following a volcanic eruption

4 POINT CLUE George Bush was laid low after choking on a pretzel

3 POINT CLUE Paula Radcliffe won the London Marathon at her first attempt

2 POINT CLUE Bindaree won the Grand National

1 POINT CLUE The Queen Mother died in April of this year

NAME THE MYSTERY MAN

5 POINT CLUE This mystery man was born in the state of Virginia and as a boy he displayed a keen interest in maths at elementary school. When he was just sixteen years of age he began working as a surveyor for Lord Fairfax.

4 POINT CLUE He was born to a farming family in 1732 and died from a throat infection on December 14, 1799. His death was mourned throughout the USA.

3 POINT CLUE In 1754 as a Lieutenant Colonel he fought in the French and Indian War and in 1775 he was elected Commander In Chief of the Continental Army.

2 POINT CLUE Nicknamed 'Father of his country', his head can be viewed on the US landmark of Mount Rushmore.

1 POINT CLUE On April 30, 1789 he became the first President of the USA.

ANSWER
GEORGE WASHINGTON

NAME THE COUNTRY

5 POINT CLUE This country has an area of 582,650 square kilometres and a coastline that is 536 kilometres long. In 2001 its population was estimated at 30,765,916.

4 POINT CLUE Major towns and cities in this country include Wajir, Lamu, Garissa, Marsabit and Mombassa.

3 POINT CLUE This country was formerly called British East Africa and has two official languages, English and Kiswahili.

2 POINT CLUE The Great Rift Valley can be found in this country that forms borders with Ethiopia, Uganda, Tanzania, Sudan and Somalia and forms a coastline with the Indian Ocean.

1 POINT CLUE The capital city of this African nation is Nairobi.

ANSWER
KENYA

NAME THE MYSTERY LADY

5 POINT CLUE This mystery lady, famous in the world of music, was born on August 28, 1965, and by the age of ten had appeared on TV singing her own compositions.

4 POINT CLUE In 1993 she signed a recording deal with Mercury Records; six years earlier her mother and step-father had been tragically killed in a car accident.

3 POINT CLUE She was born Eileen Edwards in Canada, and her first album release in 1995 earned her a Grammy Award.

2 POINT CLUE She shot to international stardom on the release of her third album *Come On Over* in 1997, which spawned eight hit singles.

1 POINT CLUE Two of those singles were entitled 'That Don't Impress Me Much' and 'Man, I Feel Like A Woman'.

ANSWER
SHANIA TWAIN

NAME THE NOVEL

5 POINT CLUE This famous novel was first published in the 19th century and the author of the novel died in 1894 at the age of forty-four. One of the characters that featured in the novel was a servant called Redruth.

4 POINT CLUE In 1950 this novel was filmed by Disney and was the studio's first full-length live action feature. Actors who appeared in the film included Ralph Truman, Bobby Driscoll and Walter Fitzgerald.

3 POINT CLUE The novel was published in book form in 1883, although it had been originally published in serial form under the title of *The Sea Cook*.

2 POINT CLUE The novel opened in the Admiral Benbow Inn and featured the characters of Squire Trelawney, Blind Pew, Dr Livesey and Ben Gunn.

1 POINT CLUE It was written by Robert Louis Stevenson and featured a pirate villain called Long John Silver.

ANSWER
TREASURE ISLAND

NAME THE MYSTERY MAN

5 POINT CLUE This mystery man, famous in the world of sport, was born in December, 1975 at Long Beach Hospital in California. In 1996 he turned professional.

4 POINT CLUE His father was a retired army lieutenant and his mother was born in Thailand. In 1996 he was voted Sports Illustrated Sportsman Of The Year.

3 POINT CLUE The Las Vegas International was one of the first professional tournaments he won, and in 1997 he won the US Masters with a record score of 18 under par.

2 POINT CLUE In the year 2000 he became the youngest ever golfer to complete a career Grand Slam, when he won the British Open by eight strokes.

1 POINT CLUE His real first name is Eldrick, but he is better known by a name that he shares with the largest species of wild cat.

ANSWER
TIGER WOODS

NAME THE SONG

5 POINT CLUE This mystery song first became a hit single in 1967 when it reached No. 5 in the UK charts. In 1994 a cover version of the song topped the singles charts.

4 POINT CLUE The song was written in 1966 and first appeared on an album entitled *Wild Thing*.

3 POINT CLUE It was written by Reg Presley and his group The Troggs were the first act to have a hit with the song.

2 POINT CLUE This mystery song opens with the line: 'I feel it in my fingers, I feel it in my toes'.

1 POINT CLUE The pop group Wet Wet Wet had the biggest hit with this song after it featured in the romantic comedy film *Four Weddings And A Funeral*.

ANSWER
LOVE IS ALL AROUND

NAME THE MYSTERY MAN

5 POINT CLUE This mystery man was born on March 30, 1950 on the outskirts of Glasgow and in 1973 he made a 50-minute documentary film entitled *Young Mental Health*, which was voted Film of the Year by the Scottish Education Council.

4 POINT CLUE His real name is Anthony Robert MacMillan and he made an early film appearance in a movie called *Death Watch* alongside Harvey Keitel.

3 POINT CLUE He starred in the films *Mona Lisa* and *Nuns On The Run* and also appeared as a member of a rock and roll band called The Majestics in the TV series *Tutti Frutti*.

2 POINT CLUE He has appeared in two James Bond movies as a Russian Mafia lord and plays a leading character in the Harry Potter films.

1 POINT CLUE In the award-winning crime drama *Cracker* he played the role of a psychologist known by the name of Fitz.

ANSWER
ROBBIE COLTRANE

NAME THE ANIMAL

5 POINT CLUE This animal has an average lifespan of 26 years in the wild and 36 years in captivity. Its average weight is 800 kg (1760 lbs) and can reach average running speeds of up to 56 km/h per hour (35 mph).

4 POINT CLUE The female of the species has a gestation period approaching 15 months and gives birth to a calf whilst standing.

3 POINT CLUE This animal has the largest eyes of any land mammal and the species include the Serengeti, the Nigerian and the Nubian.

2 POINT CLUE The male of the species can grow to heights of 5.3 m (17 feet) and possesses a tongue 45 cm (18 in) long.

1 POINT CLUE It is the tallest of all animals and possesses seven neck vertebrae that are greatly elongated in order to support its extremely long neck.

ANSWER
A GIRAFFE

NAME THE FICTIONAL CHARACTER

5 POINT CLUE This fictional character first appeared in a book in 1946 and has friends called Toby, Henry, Duck, Bertie, Percy, Daisy, Donald and Douglas.

4 POINT CLUE This character lives on the island of Sodor and two of the many books it appears in are entitled *A Better View For Gordon* and *Choo Choo Peek-A-Boo*.

3 POINT CLUE In 1984 the books were adapted into a TV series which was narrated by Ringo Starr.

2 POINT CLUE The character was created by an Anglican clergyman called Reverend Wilbert Awdry as a way of entertaining his young son Christopher, who now writes the series.

1 POINT CLUE The original tales of this blue-coloured children's character appeared in the books entitled The Railway Series.

ANSWER
THOMAS THE TANK ENGINE

NAME THE POP GROUP

5 POINT CLUE This pop group was formed in 1965 and their first No 1 in 1967, written by Neil Diamond, was a chart topper in both the USA and the UK.

4 POINT CLUE Two of their hit albums were entitled *Headquarters* and *Pisces, Aquarius, Capricorn and Jones Ltd*. In 1968 they appeared in a movie called *Head*, which despite being written by Jack Nicholson was a major box-office flop.

3 POINT CLUE Hit records include 'DW Washburn', 'Someday Man', 'Valleri' and 'Pleasant Valley Sunday'.

2 POINT CLUE The group was formed after an advert for four insane boys appeared in the *Los Angeles Daily Variety*. The four successful applicants were called Davy, Mike, Peter and Mickey.

1 POINT CLUE The two biggest hits for this group were 'I'm A Believer' and 'Daydream Believer'.

ANSWER
THE MONKEES

NAME THE MYSTERY MAN

5 POINT CLUE This mystery man, a famous author, was born in 1947 and attended Rugby School. He went on to Cambridge University, where he majored in history, before graduating in 1968.

4 POINT CLUE In 1975 his first novel entitled *Grimus* was published, and other novels include *Shame* and *Ground Beneath Her Feet*.

3 POINT CLUE He was born in the city of Bombay and before he became a successful writer he worked on television in Pakistan.

2 POINT CLUE In 1981 his novel *Midnight's Children* won the Booker Prize and brought him international fame.

I POINT CLUE In 1989 the Ayatollah Khomeni issued a death sentence on this author following the publication of his novel *The Satanic Verses*.

ANSWER
SALMAN RUSHDIE

NAME THE AMERICAN STATE

5 POINT CLUE This American state comprises of seventy-seven counties and has a name that literally means, 'red people'. Forests cover almost a quarter of this state's area.

4 POINT CLUE It is nicknamed the Sooner State, its state flower is the mistletoe and the American buffalo is the official state animal.

3 POINT CLUE This state boasts the greatest population of American Indians. A 1990 census estimated their number at 252,420. Tulsa is one of the major cities in this state.

2 POINT CLUE On November 16, 1907 it became the 46th state of the USA and in 1955 it provided the title of a film musical.

1 POINT CLUE The zip code of this state is OK.

ANSWER
OKLAHOMA

NAME THE MYSTERY MAN

5 POINT CLUE This mystery man was born in February 1633 in London over a tailor's shop owned by his father. He died on May 26, 1703.

4 POINT CLUE In 1679 he sat in Parliament, but in that year was imprisoned in the Tower of London for six weeks, after he was charged with betraying naval secrets to the French.

3 POINT CLUE Whilst working as secretary to Edward Montagu, who later became the first Earl of Sandwich, he married a fifteen-year-old French girl called Elizabeth.

2 POINT CLUE He held the post of Secretary for Admiralty Affairs and from 1684–1686 was a member of the Royal Society. Sir Christopher Wren and Sir Isaac Newton were just two of his many notable friends.

1 POINT CLUE During the 16th century he wrote a famous diary which chronicled such events as The Great Fire of London. He ended his daily entries with the words, 'and so to bed'.

ANSWER
SAMUEL PEPYS

NAME THE NOVEL

5 POINT CLUE This novel was first published in 1846 and opens with the line, '1801 – I have just returned from a visit to my landlord, the solitary neighbour that I shall be troubled with'.

4 POINT CLUE The novel is primarily narrated by Mr Lockwood and Nellie Dean, the housekeeper of Thrushcross Grange.

3 POINT CLUE The novel is set in Yorkshire and other characters include Edgar and Isabella Linton.

2 POINT CLUE It has been filmed several times with versions starring Laurence Olivier in 1939, Timothy Dalton in 1970 and Ralph Fiennes in 1992. In 1978 it provided the subject and inspiration for a No. 1 hit single.

1 POINT CLUE It was written by Emily Bronte and tells of an illicit romance between Heathcliff and Catherine Earnshaw.

ANSWER
WUTHERING HEIGHTS

NAME THE MYSTERY MAN

5 POINT CLUE This mystery man famous in the world of contemporary music was born October 17, 1972 in Kansas, before moving to Detroit with his mother when he was twelve years old.

4 POINT CLUE Early in his career he formed one half of a duo called Soul Intent and in 1996 he released his solo debut album entitled *Infinite*.

3 POINT CLUE In 1999 he was arrested on two occasions on weapons charges, won a host of awards at the MTV Awards and was sued by his mother.

2 POINT CLUE His real name is Marshall Mathers and he is also known by the name of The Slim Shady after one of his album releases.

1 POINT CLUE This controversial rap artist is noted for appearing on stage wearing an ice hockey goal-keeper's mask and wielding a chainsaw.

ANSWER
EMINEM

NAME THE ANIMAL

5 POINT CLUE This mystery animal feeds on grass and herbs and is a protected species, its dwindling numbers due to them having been hunted for their skins and used for food.

4 POINT CLUE It is found primarily on the Savannah of Africa and comprises of several species including, the Grevy's, the Plains and the Mountain. This animal can reach a running speed of up to 64 km/h (40 mph).

3 POINT CLUE The quagga, declared extinct in the late 19th century, was a sub-species of this animal.

2 POINT CLUE The female of the species gives birth to a foal after a gestation period of up to thirteen months. The young are capable of running within fourteen minutes of birth.

1 POINT CLUE This equine creature is noted for its black and white striped coat.

ANSWER
A ZEBRA

NAME THE MYSTERY MAN

5 POINT CLUE This mystery man famous in the world of sport was born on September 9, 1965 in London. At the age of seventeen he became the World Junior Champion and he turned professional in 1989. His first fight as a pro resulted in a second-round stoppage of Al Malcolm.

4 POINT CLUE In April 1992 he captured the Commonwealth title and in 1993, in a much-hyped fight, he stopped Frank Bruno in the seventh round.

3 POINT CLUE At the 1988 Olympics he represented Canada and won a gold medal in the Super Heavyweight division beating Riddick Bowe in the final.

2 POINT CLUE In September 1994 he lost his WBC title to Oliver McCall but managed to regain it in February 1997 in a rematch.

1 POINT CLUE In November 1999 he unified the world titles when he comprehensively out-pointed Evander Holyfield, having previously met him in a controversial drawn bout.

ANSWER
LENNOX LEWIS

NAME THE SONG

5 POINT CLUE This famous song has been recorded by numerous artists including Perry Como, Frank Sinatra, Barbara Streisand, The Righteous Brothers, Louis Armstrong, Shirley Bassey, Elvis Presley and Dionne Warwick.

4 POINT CLUE It was written by Rodgers & Hammerstein during World War II and was first recorded in 1951.

3 POINT CLUE This song features in the stage and film musical *Carousel* opens with the words, 'When you walk through a storm'.

2 POINT CLUE The 1960s pop group Gerry And The Pacemakers had a huge worldwide hit with this song in 1963.

1 POINT CLUE This song was adopted by fans of Liverpool Football Club as their anthem.

ANSWER
YOU'LL NEVER WALK ALONE

NAME THE ACTOR

5 POINT CLUE He was born in the Bronx on June 3, 1925, the son of an Hungarian-born tailor. During World War II he served in the navy and was injured in action in a battle at Guam.

4 POINT CLUE After signing a seven-year contract with Universal Studios he made his film debut in a 1948 movie called *Criss Cross*.

3 POINT CLUE On film he has played Albert de Salvo and Harry Houdini and he also played the character of Danny Wilde in a 1970s TV series.

2 POINT CLUE He was born Bernard Schwartz and his more notable movies include *Some Like It Hot*, *Spartacus* and *The Defiant Ones*.

1 POINT CLUE He married the actress Janet Leigh and their daughter Jamie Lee Curtis continued the family's acting tradition.

ANSWER
TONY CURTIS

NAME THE POP GROUP

5 POINT CLUE This world-famous pop group first performed together under the name of Festfolk. A canned fish company shares the name for which they are famous and the group had to gain permission from that company to use the name.

4 POINT CLUE They last toured together in 1980 and disbanded the following year. In 1993 they released a greatest hits collection, which sold over 13 million copies worldwide.

3 POINT CLUE In 1974 they were triumphant in the Eurovision Song Contest and in 1999 this group became the subject of a stage musical that features twenty-two of their songs.

2 POINT CLUE They have topped the charts all over the world with songs such as 'Dancing Queen', 'Take A Chance On Me' and 'Fernando'.

1 POINT CLUE The members of this Swedish foursome are called Bjorn, Benny, Agnetha and Ani-Frid.

ANSWER
ABBA

NAME THE FAMOUS LADY

5 POINT CLUE This mystery lady was born on October 13, 1925. She became a Master of Arts at Oxford University and also gained a degree in natural science at Somerville College in Oxford.

4 POINT CLUE She went on to work for an industrial firm as a research chemist whilst she was studying to become a barrister. She was called to the Bar in 1954 and she specialised in taxation law.

3 POINT CLUE In 1990 she was awarded the Order of Merit by the Queen and two years later she became the Baroness of Kesteven.

2 POINT CLUE Her middle name is Hilda and her maiden name is Roberts. In 1959 she was elected to the House of Commons as the member for Finchley.

I POINT CLUE In 1979 she became the first female Prime Minister of Great Britain.

ANSWER
MARGARET THATCHER

NAME THE CITY

5 POINT CLUE This city is known as the Queen of the Mediterranean. One of its famous citizens was the architect Gaudi who designed many of its buildings.

4 POINT CLUE Famous buildings in the city include the Calatrava Tower and a statue of Christopher Columbus. The El Prat de Llobregat Airport serves this city.

3 POINT CLUE This city is the capital of a region called Catalonia and has two official languages, Catalan and Castilian.

2 POINT CLUE In 1992, Freddie Mercury and Montserrat Cabelle collaborated on a hit single to celebrate this city hosting the Summer Olympics.

1 POINT CLUE The Nou Camp Stadium is the home to this city's famous football team that was once managed by Terry Venables.

ANSWER
BARCELONA

NAME THE MYSTERY MAN

5 POINT CLUE This mystery man was born in New York in 1937 and in 1971 he gained a degree in business administration at the George Washington University.

4 POINT CLUE In 1958 he was commissioned as a second Lieutenant in the US Army and he was wounded in action during the Vietnam War.

3 POINT CLUE For his role in the Gulf War he was awarded a Congressional Gold Medal.

2 POINT CLUE In Ronald Reagan's administration he served as the security advisor to the President and in 1989 he became the first African American to be appointed the Chairman of the Joint Chief of Staffs.

1 POINT CLUE On December 16, 2000 George W Bush nominated this man to become the Secretary of State and he was officially sworn in on January 20 the following year.

ANSWER
COLIN POWELL

NAME THE FAMOUS FILM

5 POINT CLUE This famous film, a huge box-office success, featured the characters of Mary, Keys, Michael, Steve and Tyler amongst others.

4 POINT CLUE It was released in 1982 and despite being nominated for nine Oscars it only won minor awards for sound, music and visual effects.

3 POINT CLUE The film was written by Melissa Mathison, who married the actor Harrison Ford. He played a cameo role as a school principal in the film, but his scenes were removed from the final cut.

2 POINT CLUE The cast list of this film included Drew Barrymore, Peter Coyote, Dee Wallace and Henry Thomas.

1 POINT CLUE This film told the story of an alien attempting to phone home.

ANSWER
ET

NAME THE MYSTERY MAN

5 POINT CLUE This mystery man was born Grigori Effimovich in the 19th century and died in the 20th century.

4 POINT CLUE He has been played on film many times including portrayals by Gert Frobe, Lionel Barrymore, Christopher Lee, Tom Baker and Alan Rickman.

3 POINT CLUE He died in 1916, eventually drowning in the River Neva after being stabbed, shot, poisoned, battered and strangled.

2 POINT CLUE He was the son of a peasant and joined a monastery at the age of 16. He went on to become a powerful figure in the court of Czar Nicholas II.

I POINT CLUE He was nicknamed the Mad Monk and according to the pop group Boney M, he was Russia's greatest love machine.

ANSWER
RASPUTIN

NAME THE MYSTERY MAN

5 POINT CLUE This mystery man was born in London in 1944 and moved to the USA with his family when he was five years of age. In 1968 he graduated from Northwestern University with a Law Degree.

4 POINT CLUE He worked as a campaign aide for the politician Robert Kennedy and following the assassination of Kennedy he accepted a job at a law firm in the state of Ohio.

3 POINT CLUE In the 1980s he began working on television as the anchorman for the WLWT-TV station and his performances earned him several Emmy Awards.

2 POINT CLUE In 1977 he was elected as Mayor for Cincinnati, a post he resigned in 1981.

1 POINT CLUE He is most famous for hosting a talk show in which the guests frequently come to blows.

ANSWER
JERRY SPRINGER

NAME THE MYSTERY SINGER

5 POINT CLUE This mystery man, a famous name in the world of pop music, was born on February 25, 1943 and early in his singing career he performed with a group called the Les Stuart Quartet.

4 POINT CLUE Although he will be best remembered as a member of a famous group, his solo albums include *Extra Texture*, *Cloud Nine*, *Living In The Material World* and *Dark Horse*.

3 POINT CLUE He died of cancer on November 29, 2001 and during his lifetime he wrote a song that Frank Sinatra described as the greatest love song of the last forty years.

2 POINT CLUE He was the co-founder of the film production company Handmade Films and was also a member of the Traveling Wilburys.

I POINT CLUE This member of the Beatles had a solo chart-topping single with the song 'My Sweet Lord'.

ANSWER
GEORGE HARRISON

NAME THE MYSTERY MAN

5 POINT CLUE This mystery man was born in the state of New Jersey in 1930. He graduated with honours from the West Point Military Academy and during the Korean War he piloted Sabre jets in numerous combat missions.

4 POINT CLUE In 1974 he wrote his autobiography entitled *Return To Earth* and several years later he established his own company called Starcraft Enterprises.

3 POINT CLUE In 1969 he was presented with the Presidential Medal of Freedom. His mother had the rather prophetic maiden name of Marion Moon.

2 POINT CLUE His first two names are Edwin Eugene, although he is better known by a four-letter nickname.

1 POINT CLUE In 1969 Neil Armstrong became the first man to set foot on the moon. This mystery man became the second on that same Apollo mission.

ANSWER
BUZZ ALDRIN

NAME THE MYSTERY SPORTS STAR

5 POINT CLUE This mystery lady, a famous name in the world of sport, was born on June 14, 1969 and in 1988 she won a gold medal at the Seoul Olympic Games.

4 POINT CLUE She turned professional at the tender age of thirteen and won over 100 championships in her playing career before announcing her retirement in 1999.

3 POINT CLUE In 1987 she won her first Grand Slam singles title and the following year completed the Grand Slam of the US Open, the French Open, the Australian Open and Wimbledon.

2 POINT CLUE Her middle name is Maria and in 1993 she was the opponent of Monica Seles, during the game in which Monica was stabbed by a deranged fan.

1 POINT CLUE She was born in Germany and in 2001 she married fellow tennis star Andre Agassi in a ceremony in Las Vegas.

ANSWER
STEFFI GRAFF

NAME THE MYSTERY YEAR

5 POINT CLUE In this year the USA women's soccer team won The World Cup and the world population reached the 6 billion milestone.

4 POINT CLUE A computer virus called Melissa wreaked havoc through the Internet and Vladimir Putin was appointed Prime Minister of Russia.

3 POINT CLUE This year saw the deaths of John F Kennedy Jnr and the golfer Payne Stewart who were both killed in plane crashes. Other deaths included King Hussein of Jordan and the former baseball star Joe di Maggio.

2 POINT CLUE In February of this year Bill Clinton was acquitted by the Senate on impeachment charges and Nelson Mandela retired as President of South Africa.

1 POINT CLUE In this year Prince Edward tied the knot with Sophie Rhys-Jones and Manchester United won an unprecedented treble of League title, FA Cup and European Champions Cup.

ANSWER
1999

NAME THE MYSTERY FILM STAR

5 POINT CLUE This mystery film star was born on August 25, 1930 and his early films included *No Road Back*, *Lets Make Up* and *Time Lock*. He was also one of the many stars of the World War II epic *A Bridge Too Far*.

4 POINT CLUE On July 5, 2000 he received a knighthood. Fifty years earlier he was contestant number 24 in the Mr Universe contest in which he was eventually placed third.

3 POINT CLUE His real first name is Thomas, and in 1993 a biography entitled *Neither Shaken Nor Stirred* was written about him.

2 POINT CLUE On film he has played Richard the Lionheart, Robin Hood and the father of Indiana Jones. He has also starred in big screen versions of *The Avengers*, *Highlander* and *The Untouchables*.

I POINT CLUE He starred as James Bond in seven films, the first being *Dr No*, before saying farewell to the role of 007 in the film *Never Say Never Again*.

ANSWER
SEAN CONNERY

NAME THE MYSTERY ISLAND

5 POINT CLUE This island country has an area of 110,861 square kilometres (42,803 square miles), which is divided into fourteen provinces.

4 POINT CLUE Its national flag has blue and white horizontal bands with a red triangle and a five-pointed star. The title of this country's national anthem translates into English as 'To Battle, Men Of Bayamo'.

3 POINT CLUE Major towns on the island include Cienfuegos, Guantanamo and Santa Clara. The monetary unit on this island is the peso, which is divided into 100 centavos.

2 POINT CLUE In 1959 this island witnessed a revolution led by Fidel Castro that overthrew the government led by General Batista.

1 POINT CLUE This is the largest island in the Caribbean and its capital city is Havana.

ANSWER
CUBA

NAME THE MYSTERY MAN

5 POINT CLUE This mystery man was born in 1885 and trained to be a teacher at Nottingham University College before becoming a famous name in the world of literature.

4 POINT CLUE In 1914 he married Frieda von Richthofen Weekley and three years later he wrote a collection of poems entitled *Look! We Have Come Through!*

3 POINT CLUE He died in 1930 and his lesser-known novels include *The Lost Girl*, *Kangaroo* and *The Plumed Serpent*.

2 POINT CLUE His first two names are David Herbert and one of his more famous novels was the subject of a controversial court case.

1 POINT CLUE This famous author penned the novels *Lady Chatterley's Lover* and *Sons And Lovers*.

ANSWER
DH LAWRENCE

NAME THE MYSTERY TV PROGRAMME

5 POINT CLUE This mystery TV programme debuted in 1978 and ran for thirteen years encompassing over 350 episodes. The actor Brad Pitt had a bit-part in the series before becoming a Hollywood superstar.

4 POINT CLUE Stars who have appeared in the programme include Ian McShane, Joel Grey, Lesley-Anne Down, George Kennedy, Kate Mulgrew, Christopher Atkins, Howard Keel and John Beck.

3 POINT CLUE Characters in the series included Angelica Nero, April Stevens, Ben Stivers, Don Lockwood, Katherine Wentworth, Jeff Farraday and Mitch Cooper.

2 POINT CLUE An episode that was shown in 1980 received record viewing figures, as fans tuned in to discover that Kristen Shepard had pulled the trigger.

1 POINT CLUE This American TV soap featured dirty double dealings in the oil business and starred Larry Hagman as the ruthless JR Ewing.

ANSWER
DALLAS

NAME THE MYSTERY MAN

5 POINT CLUE This mystery man was born on New Year's Day, 1895 in Washington DC. As a youngster he made money by delivering groceries, earning the nickname of Speed, because he realised that the faster he made the deliveries the more money he could earn.

4 POINT CLUE He was a member of the Central High School debating team which honed his public speaking skills, and he went on to enrol at the George Washington University in a work study programme for government employees.

3 POINT CLUE He later worked for the Justice Department, earning $900 a year as a clerk. A few months later his salary had doubled after he was promoted to the post of attorney.

2 POINT CLUE His first name was John, though he seldom used it, and Bob Hoskins played him on film in the movie *Nixon*.

1 POINT CLUE In 1924 he was named Director of the FBI, a post he held under eight Presidents until the time of his death in 1972.

ANSWER
J EDGAR HOOVER

NAME THE MYSTERY LADY

5 POINT CLUE This mystery lady was born at the end of the 16th century and was kidnapped early in the 17th century by Captain Samuel Argall.

4 POINT CLUE According to the legend, in 1607 she saved the life of Captain John Smith, when he was about to be beaten to death.

3 POINT CLUE Her name, when translated into English, means 'playful, frolicsome little girl'. In 1614 she converted to Christianity, was re-christened Rebecca and married a tobacco planter called John Rolfe.

2 POINT CLUE She died at the age of 22 and is buried in a churchyard in Gravesend, England.

1 POINT CLUE The story of this Indian Princess was filmed by the Disney Studios and was the first Disney animation to be based on a true story.

ANSWER
POCAHONTAS

NAME THE MYSTERY MAN

5 POINT CLUE This mystery man was born in Dublin in 1769, the son of the Earl of Mornington. He was educated at Eton School and went on to train at a military school in Angers.

4 POINT CLUE In 1806 he was elected MP for Rye in Sussex and on entering the House of Commons he took up the post of Irish Secretary.

3 POINT CLUE His real name is Arthur Wellesley; he died in 1852 and is buried in St Paul's Cathedral.

2 POINT CLUE In 1828 he became Prime Minister and with Robert Peel as his Home Secretary he helped to re-organise the Metropolitan Police Force.

1 POINT CLUE He was in command of the forces that defeated Napoleon Bonaparte at the Battle of Waterloo in 1815.

ANSWER
THE DUKE OF WELLINGTON

NAME THE MYSTERY BUILDING

5 POINT CLUE An estimated 20,000 workers were employed daily in the construction of this mystery building that stands over 55 m high and was completed in the 17th century.

4 POINT CLUE When entering the building, one's shoes must be removed or shoe covers must be worn. Inside are a number of tombs above which is a Cairene lamp which burns permanently.

3 POINT CLUE The name of this building literally means Crown Palace, and it was built in the memory of Arjumarid Bano Begum who died in 1630.

2 POINT CLUE This building is located in the city of Agra and stands on the banks of the Jamuna River.

1 POINT CLUE Described as one of the eight modern wonders of the world, this white marble palace was built in India at an estimated cost of 32 million rupees.

ANSWER
THE TAJ MAHAL

NAME THE MYSTERY SINGER

5 POINT CLUE This mystery lady, a famous name in the world of music, was born in Memphis on March 25, 1942. Her first recordings as a teenager were on the Checker Record label and comprised of hymns that were recorded at her father's church.

4 POINT CLUE In 1980 she played the singing waitress in the cult movie *The Blues Brothers* starring John Belushi and Dan Aykroyd.

3 POINT CLUE Hit records for this singer include 'Everyday People', 'Spanish Harlem', 'Baby I Love You', 'A Rose Is Still A Rose' and 'Think'.

2 POINT CLUE In 1987 she recorded a song with George Michael entitled 'I Knew You Were Waiting', which topped the charts in both the UK and USA.

1 POINT CLUE She acquired the nickname of The Queen of Soul, and had a huge worldwide hit with the song 'I Say A Little Prayer'.

ANSWER
ARETHA FRANKLIN

NAME THE MYSTERY YEAR

5 POINT CLUE In this year the President of Egypt and the Prime Minister of Israel shared the Nobel Peace Prize. This year also saw the release of the film sequel *Jaws II* which was advertised with the publicity blurb, 'Just when you thought it was safe to go back in the water'.

4 POINT CLUE Keith Moon, the drummer with the rock group The Who, died in this year of a suspected drug overdose and Leon Spinx shocked the boxing world by relieving Muhammed Ali of his World Heavyweight title.

3 POINT CLUE Bjorn Borg won the Men's Singles at Wimbledon beating Jimmy Connors in the final in straight sets. The FA Cup in this year was won by underdogs Ipswich Town who beat Arsenal 1–0 in the final.

2 POINT CLUE Hit records of this year included 'Take A Chance On Me' by Abba and 'Wuthering Heights' by Kate Bush, whilst songs from the hit movie of the year, *Grease*, dominated the summer charts.

1 POINT CLUE This year saw Argentina as host nation winning football's World Cup, beating Holland in the final.

ANSWER
1978

NAME THE MYSTERY SPORTS STAR

5 POINT CLUE This mystery man, a famous name in the world of sport, was born on April 9, 1971 and in 1986 he enrolled at the Jim Russell Racing Drivers School.

4 POINT CLUE In 1994 whilst driving Indy Cars he was named Rookie of the Year after finishing in 6th place in the championships. The following year at the age of 24 he became the youngest ever Indy Car Champion.

3 POINT CLUE He was born in Quebec and made his debut in Formula One in 1996, winning a total of four Grand Prix races that year.

2 POINT CLUE His father Gilles was also a famous driver and he was tragically killed in an accident whilst driving in a qualification race for the Belgian Grand Prix.

1 POINT CLUE In 1997 this sports star became Formula One World Champion, driving for the Williams team, and in doing so became the first Canadian to lift the title.

ANSWER
JACQUES VILLENEUVE

NAME THE MYSTERY FILM STAR

5 POINT CLUE This mystery lady was born on the island of Hawaii on June 20, 1967 and in 1983 she won her first professional acting roles in the films *Bush Christmas* and *BMX Bandits*.

4 POINT CLUE On film she has played the wife of Sam Neill in the movie *Dead Calm* and the pregnant wife of Michael Keaton in the film *My Life*.

3 POINT CLUE In 1998 she appeared naked on stage in the critically acclaimed theatre production called *The Blue Room*.

2 POINT CLUE She played the character of Dr Chase Meridian in the film *Batman Forever* and in 2001 she recorded the song 'Somethin' Stupid' with Robbie Williams.

1 POINT CLUE In August 2001 she divorced the actor Tom Cruise after being married to him for almost eleven years.

ANSWER
NICOLE KIDMAN

NAME THE MYSTERY POP GROUP

5 POINT CLUE This pop group formed in 1971 and signed to the Asylum Record label that year. They released their debut album in 1972, which included the track 'Witchy Woman'.

4 POINT CLUE The group were originally formed as a four-piece band, the four meeting when they became members of Linda Ronstadt's backing band. They became a five-piece group when Don Felder was added to the line-up.

3 POINT CLUE Hit albums include *On The Border*, *The Long Run*, *Desperado* and a live album entitled *Hell Freezes Over*.

2 POINT CLUE Various members of the band have also enjoyed solo success including Joe Walsh, who had hits with 'Rocky Mountain Way' and 'Life's Been Good' and Glenn Frey whose biggest solo hit 'The Heat Is On' featured in the film *Beverly Hills Cop*.

I POINT CLUE This American country rock group named themselves after a bird of prey and had a huge worldwide hit album with *Hotel California*.

ANSWER
THE EAGLES

NAME THE MYSTERY MAN

5 POINT CLUE This mystery man, although born of British parents, was born in the city of Bloemfontein in South Africa on January 3, 1892. Following the death of his father he returned to England with his family to live in the West Midlands.

4 POINT CLUE This mystery man is a former professor of the Anglo-Saxon language at Oxford University and he went on to become a famous name in the world of literature.

3 POINT CLUE The rock group Marillion took their name from the title of the book Silmarillion which was written by this mystery man.

2 POINT CLUE His first names are John Ronald Reuel. He died on September 2, 1973 and has had several stories published posthumously, including the children's tale *Mr Bliss*.

1 POINT CLUE The most famous work of this author is *Lord Of The Rings*.

ANSWER
JRR TOLKIEN

NAME THE MYSTERY FILM

5 POINT CLUE This Oscar-winning mystery film includes the characters of Colonel Pickering, Freddie Eynsford-Hill, Erza D Wallingford and a maid called Mrs Pearce.

4 POINT CLUE This film was released in 1964 and was nominated for 12 Oscars, winning eight including Best Film and Best Director for George Cukor.

3 POINT CLUE This film is a famous musical that includes the songs 'With A Little Bit Of Luck', 'The Street Where You Live' and 'W'ouldn't It Be Loverly'.

2 POINT CLUE George Bernard Shaw wrote the play *Pygmalion*, on which this film was based.

1 POINT CLUE The two lead characters in the film, Professor Higgins and Eliza Doolittle, were played by Rex Harrison and Audrey Hepburn.

ANSWER
MY FAIR LADY

NAME THE MYSTERY MAN

5 POINT CLUE This mystery man was born on October 21, 1831 and as a child he moved with his family to St Petersburg where he was educated, becoming fluent in five different languages.

4 POINT CLUE He became an extremely wealthy man owning patents on over 350 inventions. In 1864 his brother Emil was killed in an explosion.

3 POINT CLUE He was born in the Swedish capital of Stockholm and died in the Italian town of San Remo on December 10, 1896 after developing angina pectoris.

2 POINT CLUE In 1866 he invented dynamite and set up companies and laboratories to manufacture his invention in more than twenty countries around the world.

1 POINT CLUE When he died he left $9 million in his will to finance annual prizes in his name in the fields of science, literature and peace.

ANSWER
ALFRED NOBEL

NAME THE MYSTERY COUNTRY

5 POINT CLUE This mystery country has a total area of 30,510 sq km and a population exceeding ten and a quarter million. Since 1830 this country has been a constitutional monarchy.

4 POINT CLUE Since January 1, 2002 the official currency of this country has been the Euro and this country's flag comprises of three stripes of yellow, black and red.

3 POINT CLUE In King Albert II was crowned King of this country, which forms a 450-km long border with the Netherlands.

2 POINT CLUE Towns and cities in this country include Antwerp, Liege, Ghent, Bergen and Bruges.

1 POINT CLUE The capital city of this European country is Brussels.

ANSWER
BELGIUM

NAME THE MYSTERY MAN

5 POINT CLUE This mystery man, a famous actor, was born in 1947 and was raised in the US state of Arizona. Early in his acting career he played a villain in an American soap opera entitled *Somerset*.

4 POINT CLUE He made his film debut in 1979 in a movie called *The Onion Field* in which he played a policeman who was murdered.

3 POINT CLUE He has appeared in a number of sitcoms on TV including *Becker*, in which he plays a bad-tempered doctor, and *Ink*, in which he co-stars with his wife Mary Steenburger.

2 POINT CLUE On TV he played the title role in the mini series *Gulliver's Travels* and his other films include *Loch Ness*, *Saving Private Ryan* and *Three Men And A Baby*.

1 POINT CLUE This actor played the role of Sam Malone in the popular US sitcom *Cheers*.

ANSWER
TED DANSON

NAME THE MYSTERY MAN

5 POINT CLUE This mystery man, the son of the seventh Baron of Westmeath, was born in Wales in 1888, and following his graduation from Oxford University he worked as an assistant for the British Museum on an excavation in Iraq.

4 POINT CLUE During World War I he took up a post in the military intelligence department in Cairo and in the 1920s he worked as a political advisor to Winston Churchill.

3 POINT CLUE He wrote two autobiographical books, one of which was entitled *The Mint*, which told of his experiences as an RAF recruit. His other book, entitled *Seven Pillars of Wisdom* was an account of his service during the Arab revolt.

2 POINT CLUE His first two names are Thomas Edward and in 1935 he died after falling off his motorcycle.

1 POINT CLUE In 1962 he was played by Peter O'Toole in an award-winning film directed by David Lean.

ANSWER
T E LAWRENCE AKA LAWRENCE OF ARABIA

NAME THE MYSTERY YEAR

5 POINT CLUE In this year the Martin Luther King National Holiday was celebrated for the first time in the USA, and the Statue of Liberty in New York celebrated her 100th birthday.

4 POINT CLUE Desmond Tutu became Archbishop of Cape Town and December of this year saw Halley's Comet make its 75-yearly visit.

3 POINT CLUE Famous people who died in this year include the former British Prime Minister Harold Macmillan, pop star Phil Lynott and the film stars James Cagney and Cary Grant.

2 POINT CLUE In this year Mike Tyson became the youngest ever heavyweight boxing world champion and the American space shuttle *Challenger* exploded seconds after take-off.

1 POINT CLUE This year also witnessed the nuclear Chernobyl disaster and Maradona's controversial 'hand of God' goal in the World Cup finals.

ANSWER
1986

Name the Mystery Pop Star

5 POINT CLUE This mystery lady was born on March 26, 1944 in the US state of Michigan, and early in her singing career was a member of a group called The Primettes.

4 POINT CLUE She has been a recording artist for over 40 years and hit albums include *Eaten Alive*, *Baby Its Me* and *Silk Electric*.

3 POINT CLUE In 1973 she recorded a duet album with the soul star Marvin Gaye. Other artists she has collaborated with include Michael Jackson and Lionel Richie.

2 POINT CLUE On film she played the jazz singer Billie Holliday in *Lady Sings The Blues* and she also played the role of Dorothy in a modern-day version of *The Wizard of Oz* entitled *The Wiz*.

1 POINT CLUE In 1970 she left The Supremes to forge a solo career that has include the smash hit records 'I'm Still Waiting' and 'Chain Reaction'.

ANSWER
DIANA ROSS

Name the Mystery City

5 POINT CLUE This mystery city was originally called Fort Dearborn and in the 1830s had a population of just over 4000. Today the population of this city is approaching 3 million.

4 POINT CLUE The first ever skyscraper in the world, the Home Insurance Building, was built in this city in 1885 by the architect Major William Le Baron Jenney.

3 POINT CLUE In 1871 this city fell victim to a huge fire that claimed 300 lives. The major airport in this city is called the O'Hare International Airport.

2 POINT CLUE The name of this city is also the title of an award winning stage musical that tells the story of a chorus girl called Roxie Hart.

1 POINT CLUE This city is located in the American state of Illinois, is nicknamed The Windy City and is home to the Sears Tower.

ANSWER
CHICAGO

Name the Mystery Sports Star

5 POINT CLUE This mystery lady was born in the town of Bunnvale in the state of New Jersey on August 4, 1958. She has been described as the greatest ever runner who never won an Olympic medal.

4 POINT CLUE In the late 1960s she moved with her family to a suburb of Los Angeles and while she was still a teenager she broke the world records for the women's 800 m and 1000 m.

3 POINT CLUE In 1982 at her first attempt at the distance of 10,000 m she set a new world record time of 31 minutes 35.23 seconds. The Associated Press subsequently named her Female Athlete of The Year.

2 POINT CLUE In 1983 at the World Athletics Championships she won gold medals in the 1500 m and the 3000 m. In 1985 she married a British discus thrower and her first child was born the following year.

1 POINT CLUE At the 1984 Olympics she was involved in an infamous incident when she collided with Zola Budd and fell in the 3000 m final.

ANSWER
MARY DECKER AKA MARY DECKER SLANEY

Name the Mystery Play

5 POINT CLUE This famous play was first adapted into a Hollywood screen production in 1936 in a film that starred Leslie Howard, Norma Shearer, John Barrymore and Basil Rathbone.

4 POINT CLUE The character list of this play includes Gregory, Sampson, Abraham, Tybalt, Paris, Benvolio and Mercutio.

3 Point Clue This play was written in 1595 and has inspired many films including a 1996 version in which the title roles were played by Leonardo DiCaprio and Claire Danes.

2 POINT CLUE This play is set in Verona and tells the story of two feuding families called the Montagues and the Capulets.

1 POINT CLUE This famous tragic love story was written by William Shakespeare and the musical *West Side Story* was based on this play.

ANSWER
ROMEO AND JULIET

Name the Mystery Film Star

5 POINT CLUE This mystery man, a Hollywood legend, was born in Nebraska on May 10, 1899 and died in June 1987 after a bout of pneumonia.

4 POINT CLUE He made his film debut in 1933 in a movie called *Dancing Lady*. Other films he has appeared in include *The Sky's The Limit*, *Holiday Inn*, *Royal Wedding* and *You'll Never Get Rich*.

3 POINT CLUE In 1975 he received an Oscar nomination for his role as a conman in the disaster movie *The Towering Inferno*.

2 POINT CLUE He was born Frederick Austerlitz and a studio talent scout once said of him, 'Can't act. Can't sing. Slightly bald. Can dance a little'.

1 POINT CLUE In 1933 he made the film *Flying Down To Rio*, the first of many films he made with his dancing partner Ginger Rogers.

ANSWER
FRED ASTAIRE

Name the Mystery Man

5 POINT CLUE This mystery man was born in 1863 and died in 1947. During his lifetime he was a close friend of Thomas Alva Edison and actually bought a holiday home next door to a lodge owned by Edison.

4 POINT CLUE As a teenager he worked as an apprentice machinist by day and as a watch repairer by night. In 1903 he set up a world-famous company.

3 POINT CLUE He married Clara Jane Bryant and their only son was named Edsel after a boyhood friend.

2 POINT CLUE When he was seventeen years of age he began working at the Michigan Car Company and later in his life he is credited with saying, 'You can have any colour you want as long as it's black'.

1 POINT CLUE He is undoubtedly the most famous name in motor car manufacturing and was responsible for the Model-T car affectionately known as Tin Lizzie.

ANSWER
HENRY FORD

Name the Mystery Animal

5 POINT CLUE At birth this mystery animal weighs just over 2 kg and at maturity the males reach weights of up to 165 kg. The females of the species are approximately half the weight of the males.

4 POINT CLUE These animals are primarily vegetarians and gather in social groups that are known as harems.

3 POINT CLUE Species of this animal include the Eastern lowland, the Western lowland, the Cross River and the Mountain.

2 POINT CLUE In 1978, Diane Fossey, once played on film by Sigourney Weaver, set up a fund dedicated to the conservation of this animal.

1 POINT CLUE This animal is the largest of the great apes and films made about this creature include *King Kong* and *Mighty Joe Young*.

ANSWER
GORILLA

Name the Mystery Man

5 POINT CLUE This mystery man was born in 1908 and studied languages at universities in Munich and Geneva. He was born into a wealthy family and his father called Valentine died in World War I. The obituary for his father appeared in the Times newspaper and was written by Winston Churchill.

4 POINT CLUE During World War II this mystery man worked for the British Naval intelligence and after the war he worked as the foreign correspondent manager for the Sunday Times.

3 POINT CLUE He died in 1964 leaving a legacy of novels that were adapted into many films, some of which starred Christopher Lee, Dick Van Dyke, David Niven and Sean Connery.

2 POINT CLUE He owned a house on the island of Jamaica called Goldeneye and the author Alistair MacLean once said rather scathingly that this famous man 'relies on sex, sadism and snobbery'.

1 POINT CLUE This author was the man who created the character of James Bond.

ANSWER
IAN FLEMING

Name the Mystery Year

5 POINT CLUE In this year Henry Ford instituted the five day working week at his car plants and Benny Goodman, known as the King of Swing, made his first ever record.

4 POINT CLUE In the world of sport, the golfer Bobby Jones won the British Open and the boxer Gene Tunney surprisingly beat Jack Dempsey.

3 POINT CLUE This year saw the birth of the Hollywood icon Marilyn Monroe and the deaths of the screen lover Rudolph Valentino and the escapologist Harry Houdini.

2 POINT CLUE John Logie Baird gave his first public demonstration of his mechanised television system in this year and Gertrude Ederle became the first woman to swim the English Channel.

1 POINT CLUE Princess Elizabeth, later Queen Elizabeth II, was born in this year that also witnessed the General Strike in Great Britain.

ANSWER
1926

Name the Mystery Man

5 POINT CLUE This mystery man, famous in the world of entertainment, was born in Philadelphia in 1937. In the 1960s he worked as a stand-up comedian and several albums of his comedy material earned him a number of gold discs.

4 POINT CLUE He has written several books, two of which are entitled *Childhood* and *Love And Marriage*. In 1972 he made his film debut in a movie called *Hickey And Boggs*.

3 POINT CLUE Other films that he has made include *Ghost Dad*, *The Meteor Man*, *A Piece Of The Action*, *California Suite* and *Let's Do It Again*.

2 POINT CLUE In the 1960s he co-starred in a successful sitcom with Robert Culp entitled *I Spy*.

1 POINT CLUE His most famous role is in a long running American sitcom in which he plays the character of Dr Clifford Huxtable.

ANSWER
BILL COSBY

NAME THE MYSTERY MAN

5 POINT CLUE This mystery man was born in 1859 in the slums of New York and in the US town of Fort Sumner, the town where he died, there is a museum dedicated to his life.

4 POINT CLUE At the age of fourteen he was arrested and jailed for stealing laundry and two years later he was jailed for stealing horses. He was killed in 1881 shortly after escaping from jail.

3 POINT CLUE This mystery man was played by Paul Newman in the film *The Left Handed Gun*, and by Buster Crabbe in the film *The Mysterious Rider*.

2 POINT CLUE He was born Henry McCarthy but changed his name to William H Bonney and was a member of a gang called The Regulators.

1 POINT CLUE He was also played on film by Emilio Estevez in the film *Young Guns* and he was shot and killed by Sheriff Pat Garrett.

ANSWER
BILLY THE KID

NAME THE MYSTERY COUNTRY

5 POINT CLUE This mystery country covers an area of 1,285,216 sq km and has a population of over 23 million. This country's flag is red and white and its national day is celebrated on July 28, the anniversary of its independence.

4 POINT CLUE The guerrilla terrorist group known as The Shining Path operates in this country and major cities in this country include Arequipa and Trujillo.

3 POINT CLUE The three official languages of this country are Spanish, Aymara and Quechua. The world's longest range of mountains, the Andes, runs down the length of this country.

2 POINT CLUE It was conquered in the early 16th century by Francisco Pizarro and consequently came under Spanish rule for almost 300 years. For the previous 500 years the Inca civilisation had been the dominant ruling caste in this country.

1 POINT CLUE This South American country has a coastline on the Pacific Ocean and its capital city is Lima.

ANSWER
PERU

NAME THE MYSTERY LADY

5 POINT CLUE This mystery lady, famous in the world of music, was born in Baltimore in 1915 and songs she recorded included a controversial track entitled 'Strange Fruit'.

4 POINT CLUE In the 1930s she toured with the orchestras of Count Basie and Artie Shaw before embarking on a solo career. She recorded over 200 songs in the 1930s and 1940s but never received a single royalty payment.

3 POINT CLUE Her real name is Eleanora Fagin and she was jailed for prostitution when she was still a teenager. In 1959 she was arrested on her deathbed for possession of narcotics but died before the case could come to court.

2 POINT CLUE Her own compositions included 'God Bless The Child' and 'Don't Explain'. The final album of this singer, famed for wearing white gardenia flowers in her hair, was entitled *Lady In Satin*.

1 POINT CLUE This famous jazz and blues singer was nicknamed Lady Day.

ANSWER
BILLIE HOLLIDAY

NAME THE MYSTERY MAN

5 POINT CLUE This mystery man was born on June 11, 1910 and won two Academy Awards, the first in 1956 and the second ten years later. He died in 1997 and in the last few years of his life he was embroiled in a bitter legal battle with his son over the use of the family name.

4 POINT CLUE In 1985 he was awarded the Medal of Freedom by President Reagan and in 1989 he was honoured by France with membership in the French Academy.

3 POINT CLUE The films for which he received Academy Awards were documentary films entitled *The Silent World* and *World Without Sun.*

2 POINT CLUE In 1957 he became director of the Oceanographic Museum of Monaco and he owned a research ship called *The Calypso.*

1 POINT CLUE In 1974 he established a society to protect ocean life and he is famed for his invention of the aqualung.

ANSWER
JACQUES COUSTEAU

NAME THE MYSTERY SPORTS STAR

5 POINT CLUE This famous name in the world of sport was born in the county of Staffordshire in 1915. He attended St Luke's School in the town of Hanley and in 1931 signed professional terms with his local club.

4 POINT CLUE He played for England on 54 occasions, which would have been many more but for the advent of World War II. His playing career lasted for over 30 years and when he retired from playing he went on to manage Port Vale FC.

3 POINT CLUE He was nicknamed The Wizard of Dribble and when he died in the year 2000 his ashes were buried beneath the centre circle of the Britannia Stadium, the home of Stoke City Football Club.

2 POINT CLUE In 1965 he became the first ever footballer to be knighted and he was also the first player to be voted European Footballer of the Year.

1 POINT CLUE The 1953 FA Cup final won by Blackpool was named after this famous sportsman, who was still playing top flight football on his 50th birthday.

ANSWER
SIR STANLEY MATTHEWS

NAME THE MYSTERY LADY

5 POINT CLUE This mystery lady was born on February 18, 1933, the eldest of three children in a wealthy aristocratic family. She studied philosophy, music and art at the Sarah Lawrence College in New York but dropped out of college to elope with her first husband.

4 POINT CLUE She was dubbed 'The high priestess of the happening' and her first name when translated into English means 'ocean child'.

3 POINT CLUE She has been married three times; her first husband was a composer, her second husband a film maker and her third husband a world-famous pop star.

2 POINT CLUE Her pop star husband died in 1980 and in 1995 she collaborated with her son and his rock band called Ima.

1 POINT CLUE In 1969 she married John Lennon of the Beatles.

ANSWER
YOKO ONO

NAME THE MYSTERY FILM STAR

5 POINT CLUE This mystery film star was born in California in 1956 and was educated at the California State University. His acting career began on stage at the Great Lakes Shakespeare Festival in the state of Ohio.

4 POINT CLUE He made his debut on the big screen in a 1980 film entitled *He Knows You're Alone* and from 1980 to 1982 he starred in a TV series called *Bosom Buddies*.

3 POINT CLUE Other films this actor has starred in include *Nothing In Common*, *The Money Pit*, *Volunteers* and *Splash*.

2 POINT CLUE He has co-starred with Meg Ryan in several films, the first of which was *Joe Versus The Volcano*.

1 POINT CLUE He won Best Actor Oscars in consecutive years for his roles in the films *Forrest Gump* and *Philadelphia*.

ANSWER
TOM HANKS

NAME THE MYSTERY POP GROUP

5 POINT CLUE This pop group formed in 1965 and the following year became regular performers at the newly established UFO Club in London. In 1967 they signed their first record deal with the EMI label.

4 POINT CLUE Their debut album entitled *The Piper At The Gates Of Dawn* was named after a chapter in the children's novel *Wind In The Willows*.

3 POINT CLUE Other albums include *The Final Cut*, *Animals* and *A Momentary Lapse Of Reason*. Their debut single, a hit in 1967, was entitled 'Arnold Layne'.

2 POINT CLUE In 1979 they released an album entitled *The Wall* which featured the UK's Christmas No 1 single of that year. Three years later a film starring Bob Geldof based on the album was premiered.

1 POINT CLUE The most successful album of these pioneers of progressive rock was released in 1973 with the title *Dark Side Of The Moon*.

ANSWER
PINK FLOYD

NAME THE MYSTERY MAN

5 POINT CLUE This mystery man was born in 1771 and qualified as a lawyer before declaring himself bankrupt in 1826. He died in 1832 twelve years after being created a Baronet and receiving a *knighthood*.

4 POINT CLUE In 1799 he was appointed Sheriff Depute of the county of Selkirk and early in the 19th century he set up a printing and publishing business.

3 POINT CLUE He was born in Edinburgh and embarked on a writing career in 1796. In 1802 his first major work entitled Minstrelsy of The Scottish Border was published.

2 POINT CLUE Novels he wrote include *The Talisman*, *Waverly* and a romantic novel entitled *The Lady Of The Lake*. He also penned a number of poems, the last of which was called 'The Lord Of The Isles'.

1 POINT CLUE His most famous literary creation was the heroic knight named Ivanhoe.

ANSWER
SIR WALTER SCOTT

NAME THE MYSTERY YEAR

5 POINT CLUE In this year a son was born to Michael Jackson and Debbie Rowe and in December of this year a Paris court convicted the terrorist known as Carlos the Jackal of murder.

4 POINT CLUE In the world of sport the Green Bay Packers won the Super Bowl and the Florida Marlins won the baseball World Series. At Wimbledon Pete Sampras and Martina Hingis won the men's and women's singles.

3 POINT CLUE The fashion designer Gianni Versace was murdered by Andrew Cunanan in Miami. In Britain a new novel became a bestseller. The title of this novel was *Harry Potter And The Philosopher's Stone.*

2 POINT CLUE In June of this year Hong Kong returned to Chinese rule and orbiting the Earth this year was a comet called Hale Bopp.

I POINT CLUE This year witnessed the tragic deaths of Diana, Princess of Wales and Mother Teresa.

ANSWER
1997

NAME THE MYSTERY FILM STAR

5 POINT CLUE This famous film star was born on April 7, 1964 and made his acting debut on television when he was just six years of age in a series called *Spyforce*. He made his big-screen debut in a 1990 film entitled *Blood Oath*.

4 POINT CLUE Other films that this actor has appeared in include *Virtuosity*, *The Quick And The Dead*, *No Way Back*, *Romper Stomper* and *LA Confidential*.

3 POINT CLUE In a critically acclaimed film of 2001 he played a schizophrenic maths genius called John Forbes Nash, the true story of a Nobel Prize winner.

2 POINT CLUE He was born in a suburb of Wellington, the capital of New Zealand, and early in his acting career he starred in the television soap opera *Neighbours*.

I POINT CLUE He was catapulted to international stardom after starring as a gladiator called Maximus.

ANSWER
RUSSELL CROWE

NAME THE MYSTERY BUILDING

5 POINT CLUE Construction of this mystery building began in 1171 and in 2000 a Norwegian daredevil called Arne Aarhus made news headlines by jumping off the top of this building.

4 POINT CLUE It stands next to the Duomo basilica and was once described by Mark Twain as 'the strangest structure that the world has any knowledge of'.

3 POINT CLUE There are 294 steps leading to the top of this building that overlooks the River Arno.

2 POINT CLUE This building was originally used as a bell tower and in 1990 it was closed to the public over safety fears.

1 POINT CLUE The third tier of this structure had not been completed when the building started to lean to one side because of shifting soil.

ANSWER
THE LEANING TOWER OF PISA

NAME THE MYSTERY LADY

5 POINT CLUE This mystery lady was born on June 10, 1965. She studied dance at the London Studio and formed her own dance troupe before beginning an acting career. Her early films include *Rowing With The Wind*, *Aria* and *Beyond Bedlam*.

4 POINT CLUE She was born in the county of Hampshire and co-formed a production company called Simian Films. In her first acting role in a Hollywood production she played a terrorist in the film *Passenger 57* starring Wesley Snipes.

3 POINT CLUE Some of her better-known film appearances include *Bedazzled*, *Ed TV* and *Austin Powers: International Man of Mystery*.

2 POINT CLUE She made news headlines for wearing a black Versace dress held together by safety pins at the film premier of *Four Weddings And A Funeral* and at the age of 29 she became the new face of Estee Lauder.

1 POINT CLUE Her relationship with Hugh Grant floundered when he was arrested in the company of a prostitute called Divine Brown.

ANSWER
ELIZABETH HURLEY

NAME THE FICTIONAL CHARACTER

5 POINT CLUE This mystery fictional character made his literary debut in 1920 and was first played on film in the 1930s by the actor Austin Trevor.

4 POINT CLUE He has appeared in many novels, assisted by Captain Hastings, and these include *Peril At End House*, *Cards On The Table* and *Cat Among Pigeons*.

3 POINT CLUE He first appeared in a story called *The Mysterious Affair At Styles* and the last book that featured this character was entitled *Curtain*, which was published in 1975.

2 POINT CLUE He solved many mysteries with the help of 'his little grey cells' and has been played on film by Albert Finney, Tony Randall and Peter Ustinov.

1 POINT CLUE This Belgian detective created by Agatha Christie solved *The Murder On The Orient Express*.

ANSWER
HERCULE POIROT

NAME THE MYSTERY LADY

5 POINT CLUE This mystery lady was born on June 1, 1974 and had her first brush with stardom on a television show called You *Can't Do That On Television*, in which she played the girlfriend of Matt LeBlanc.

4 POINT CLUE She became famous in the world of pop music and released her debut single entitled 'Fate Stay With Me' in 1987. In 1998 she duetted with Steve Tyler, the lead singer of Aerosmith, on a cover version of the Dobie Gray hit 'Drift Away'.

3 POINT CLUE Her first album in 1991 was only released in her native country of Canada but won her an award as Canada's most promising female artist.

2 POINT CLUE Hit singles for this singer include 'You Oughta Know', 'Hand In My Pocket', 'Ironic' and 'Head Over Feet'.

1 POINT CLUE In 1996 she received four Grammy Awards for her album *Jagged Little Pill* that sold over 20 million copies worldwide.

ANSWER
ALANIS MORISSETTE

NAME THE MYSTERY YEAR

5 POINT CLUE In this year Franklin D Roosevelt was re-elected as US President and the first successful helicopter flight was made.

4 POINT CLUE The novel *Gone With The Wind* by Margaret Mitchell was published and the Boulder Dam – later re-named the Hoover Dam – was completed.

3 POINT CLUE The BBC began the world's first television service with three hours of programmes per day and the film *Mutiny On The Bounty* won an Academy Award for Best Picture.

2 POINT CLUE The pop stars Buddy Holly and Roy Orbison were both born in this year that saw the start of the Spanish Civil War.

1 POINT CLUE Adolph Hitler opened the Berlin Olympics and Edward VIII abdicated to marry Wallis Simpson.

ANSWER
1936

NAME THE MYSTERY MAN

5 POINT CLUE This mystery man, the son of a US Congressman, was born in February 1902 in the city of Detroit and died from cancer in Hawaii in 1974.

4 POINT CLUE In 1927 he received the Congressional Medal of Honor and in 1938 he wrote *The Culture of Organs*, that told of his research with Dr Alexis Carrel that led to the development of the artificial heart.

3 POINT CLUE He left school in 1922 to enrol in a flight school. On completing his training he worked as an airmail pilot between St Louis and Chicago.

2 POINT CLUE In 1932 this mystery man's baby son was kidnapped and murdered by a man called Bruno Hauptman who was executed for this crime.

1 POINT CLUE He became the first pilot to fly solo non-stop across the Atlantic Ocean in a plane called *The Spirit of St Louis*.

ANSWER
CHARLES LINDBERGH

NAME THE MYSTERY ANIMAL

5 POINT CLUE There are over 900 different species of this animal that account for almost a quarter of all mammal species. These animals chiefly feed on insects, fruit and nectar.

4 POINT CLUE These animals belong to a family group called *Chiroptera*, which literally means 'hand wing' in the Greek language.

3 POINT CLUE In Europe this animal is a protected species under the Wild Life Order and they are mostly nocturnal, employing a navigation system known as echolocation.

2 POINT CLUE Species include the Philippines Tube-nosed, Greater Long Nosed, Bulmer's Fruit, Monkey and pippistrelle.

1 POINT CLUE This animal is the only mammal that is capable of true flight.

ANSWER
BAT

NAME THE MYSTERY MAN

5 POINT CLUE This mystery man was born in New York in 1960 and is a famous actor. His father was a Russian author and publicist for the American Jewish Community and his mother, a teacher, was born in Scotland.

4 POINT CLUE He graduated from Yale University with a degree in English literature and his first paid acting job came in a TV advert for beer. He made his film debut in 1988 in the box-office hit *Working Girl*.

3 POINT CLUE Other films he has appeared in include *Kalifornia* and *Chaplin*, and he also played the villain of the piece in the film *Beethoven*.

2 POINT CLUE In 1997 he won a Golden Globe Award for Best Actor in a TV series and in 2000 he starred opposite Minnie Driver in the romantic film comedy *Return To Me*.

1 POINT CLUE He swept to international stardom after landing the role of Fox Mulder in the supernatural TV series *The X Files*.

ANSWER
DAVID DUCHOVNY

NAME THE MYSTERY POP GROUP

5 POINT CLUE This mystery pop group were in 1978, and after winning a talent contest that year they signed a short-lived record deal with CBS Records.

4 POINT CLUE Their 1995 hit 'Hold Me Thrill Me Kiss Me Kill Me' featured on the soundtrack for the film *Batman Forever*. Other hit singles include 'Mysterious Ways', 'One' and 'Who's Gonna Ride Your Wild Horses'.

3 POINT CLUE One of their best-selling albums *The Joshua Tree* sold over 15 million records and featured such classic tracks as 'With Or Without You' and 'Where The Streets Have No Name'.

2 POINT CLUE The lead singer of the group was born Paul Hewson but is better known by a four-letter name, whilst the group's guitarist, known as The Edge, was born Dave Evans.

1 POINT CLUE Bono provides lead vocals for this group whose name comprises of a single letter and a single number.

ANSWER
U2

NAME THE MYSTERY MAN

5 POINT CLUE This mystery man, the son of a wealthy businessman, was born in the city of Chicago in September, 1875. He entered the Michigan Military Academy and later joined the US Cavalry, from which he was banished for being under-age.

4 POINT CLUE During World War II he worked as a war correspondent and five years after the war ended he died of a heart attack.

3 POINT CLUE He is a famous name in the world of literature and published his first story entitled *Under The Moons Of Mars* using the pen name of Normal Bean.

2 POINT CLUE He is primarily associated with one particular literary creation for which he wrote 28 novels. That character appeared in numerous film productions, including a Disney animation, and has had a suburb of Los Angeles named after it.

1 POINT CLUE This author created the character of Tarzan.

ANSWER
EDGAR RICE BURROUGHS

NAME THE MYSTERY CITY

5 POINT CLUE This mystery city was founded in 421 AD and in 1489 conquered the island of Cyprus. In 1516 the first ghetto in the world was established in this city.

4 POINT CLUE One of Europe's oldest film festivals, the Biennale del Cinema, is held in this city and the legendary lover Casanova was born in this city.

3 POINT CLUE This city gave its name to a South American country and Marco Polo travelled from this city to the court of Kublai Khan.

2 POINT CLUE Sights in this city include the Waldesian Church, Doge's Palace and St Mark's Square.

I POINT CLUE It has been described as one of Europe's most romantic cities, and gondoliers steer boats called gondolas on the canals that flow through this city.

ANSWER
VENICE

NAME THE MYSTERY MAN

5 POINT CLUE This mystery man was born on Christmas Day 1908 in the county of Surrey and died in Manchester in November 1999. Just before the outbreak of World War II he worked as a tap dancing teacher.

4 POINT CLUE He made his film debut as Polonius in a 1997 version of Shakespeare's *Hamlet* and also starred in a 1985 film version of Frankenstein called *The Bride*.

3 POINT CLUE His real name is Denis Charles Pratt and in a film entitled *Orlando* he played Queen Elizabeth I.

2 POINT CLUE The pop star Sting wrote the song 'An Englishman In New York' which was a tribute to this flamboyant mystery man.

1 POINT CLUE During World War II he worked as a nude model for a government-funded art school and this provided the title of his autobiography *The Naked Civil Servant*.

ANSWER
QUENTIN CRISP

NAME THE MYSTERY NOVEL

5 POINT CLUE This mystery novel opens in a fictional town called Mudfog and was the second novel of one of the world's most noted authors.

4 POINT CLUE It was first published in serial form from 1837 to 1839 and has been filmed many times, including versions starring Lon Chaney, Richard Dreyfus and Alec Guinness.

3 POINT CLUE Characters in this novel include Noah Claypole, Agnes Fleming, Edwin Leeford, Dr Losberne, Jack Dawkins, Mrs Mann and Mr Brownlow.

2 POINT CLUE This novel, set in Victorian England, tells of the first ten years of a young boy's life and features a dog called Bullseye.

1 POINT CLUE This novel was written by Charles Dickens and in 1969 was adapted into an Oscar-winning musical that featured the songs, 'Consider Yourself' and 'Food Glorious Food'.

ANSWER
OLIVER TWIST

NAME THE MYSTERY MAN

5 POINT CLUE This mystery man was born on December 21, 1879 and in 1894 he enrolled in a school called the Tiflis Theological Seminary from which he was later expelled. During his lifetime he was arrested and imprisoned on several occasions, the first time in 1902.

4 POINT CLUE He died in 1953 and he once said, "You cannot make a revolution with silk gloves".

3 POINT CLUE His real name was Iosif Vissarionovich Dzhugashvili and in 1913 he was the co-author of a book called *Marxism and The National Question*.

2 POINT CLUE In 1945 he attended the Yalta Conference with Winston Churchill and Franklin D Roosevelt.

1 POINT CLUE This Russian leader adopted a surname that means "man of steel".

ANSWER
JOSEF STALIN

NAME THE MYSTERY SINGER

5 POINT CLUE This mystery singer was born in New York in 1946 and his first job in the music industry was as a mail sorter for CBS Records.

4 POINT CLUE He has worked on the soundtracks for a number of films including *The Pebble And The Penguin* and his autobiography is entitled *Sweet Life: Advent On The Way To Paradise*.

3 POINT CLUE Hit albums for this singer include *This One's For You* and *Even Now* and early in his career he worked as the musical director for Bette Midler.

2 POINT CLUE His real name is Barry Alan Pinkus, and in the 1990s the boy band Take That covered one of his biggest hits 'Could It Be Magic'.

1 POINT CLUE He wrote the musical *Copacabana* and other notable hit records include 'Mandy' and 'I Can't Smile Without You'.

ANSWER
BARRY MANILOW

NAME THE MYSTERY MAN

5 POINT CLUE This mystery man was born in 1913 on the estate of his father's lemon farm in California. He attended Whittier College, a Quaker school, where he was appointed president of the student body.

4 POINT CLUE In 1940 he married a high school teacher called Patricia Ryan and in 1962 he lost the race to become Governor of California, joining a New York law firm a few months later.

3 POINT CLUE In 1995 a controversial film directed by Oliver Stone chronicled the life of this mystery man. In this film the Oscar-winning actor Anthony Hopkins portrayed him.

2 POINT CLUE His middle name was Millhouse and he died in 1994 with Ronald Reagan and Jimmy Carter amongst the many luminaries that attended his funeral.

1 POINT CLUE He became the 37th President of the USA and fell from grace following the Watergate scandal.

ANSWER
RICHARD NIXON

NAME THE MYSTERY FLOWER

5 POINT CLUE This flower has the scientific name of *Leontopodium alpinum* and can grow up to 30 cm tall. The heads of the flower are yellow and below the heads are spear-shaped white leaves that form a star shape.

4 POINT CLUE This flower adorns the two-cent Euro coin that came into circulation on January 1, 2002.

3 POINT CLUE The name of this flower dates back to the late 18th century and is derived from the German words for noble and white.

2 POINT CLUE It has also been known as the Flower of Salzburg and the Tyrol and is the national flower of Austria.

1 POINT CLUE This flower provided the title of a song that featured in the musical *The Sound Of Music* and was sung in the film by Captain Von Trapp.

ANSWER
EDELWEISS

NAME THE MYSTERY MAN

5 POINT CLUE This mystery man was born in the state of Oklahoma in March, 1954 and began his career in the world of entertainment at the tender age of two, working in the Kraft Theatre.

4 POINT CLUE When he was five years of age he starred in the film *The Journey* alongside Yul Brynner and went on to appear in a number of low-budget Disney films before landing a lead role in the 1973 movie *American Graffiti*.

3 POINT CLUE Other films he has appeared in include *The Spikes Gang*, *The Music Man* and *The Shootist*, the last film of John Wayne. He directed his first film when he was just 23 years of age, a 1977 film entitled *Grand Auto Theft*.

2 POINT CLUE Other films he has directed include *Cocoon*, *Splash*, *Backdraft*, *Ransom*, *Apollo 13* and *A Beautiful Mind*.

1 POINT CLUE He gained international fame with the role of Ritchie Cunningham in the US sitcom *Happy Days*.

NAME THE MYSTERY SINGER

5 POINT CLUE This mystery singer was born in Minnesota in 1941 and early in his career formed his own band called The Golden Chords. In 1989 he was inducted into the Rock and Roll Hall of Fame.

4 POINT CLUE One of his heroes and influences was the singer Woody Guthrie, and in his tribute he wrote a tune called 'Song To Woody'. His son Jakob has followed in his footsteps, being the lead singer of a group called The Wallflowers.

3 POINT CLUE In 1973 he starred in the film *Pat Garrett And Billy The Kid* and in 1994 he received a Grammy Award for the album *World Gone Wrong*.

2 POINT CLUE He was born Robert Allen Zimmerman and his many songs include 'Blowin' In The Wind', 'The Times They Are A-Changing' and 'Knockin' On Heaven's Door'.

1 POINT CLUE This folk singer took his stage name from the Welsh poet Dylan Thomas.

ANSWER
BOB DYLAN